MOVING for SENIORS

A step-by-step workbook

- *when to downsize*
- *where to move*
- *what to move*
- *how to keep it simple*
- *tips for adult children*

SMOOTH TRANSITIONS®

by Barbara H. Morris

Barbara H. Morris

About the author

Barbara H. Morris launched *SMOOTH TRANSITIONS*® in 1995 after helping several family members downsize and disperse estates.

She provides personal services to seniors and their adult family members in downsizing—from consulting to doing it all. She also gives humorous presentations on deciding to move, making it easy, and surviving the process.

Barbara Morris has helped launch some twenty-three *SMOOTH TRANSITIONS*® companies throughout the country and has trained another forty-five individuals who use different business names. She is a founding member of the National Association of Senior Move Managers.

A Louisville, Kentucky, native, she worked for twenty years in hospital public relations and is a graduate of the University of Indianapolis.

About the illustrator

Carol L. Cornette is a graphic designer and illustrator based in Louisville, Kentucky. She is a graduate of Western Kentucky University.

ISBN: 978-0-9671239-0-5

This workbook contains the author's opinion presented as suggestions and guidelines. It was developed through the experience of the author. The author assumes no liability or responsibility to any individual or entity directly or indirectly related to this workbook.

No part of this workbook may be reproduced in any form without permission of the author.

Fourth edition 2009

Text © 2009 Barbara H. Morris
Illustrations © 2009 Carol L. Cornette
All rights reserved.

MOVING FOR SENIORS: *A step-by-step workbook*

CONTENTS

Household Downsizing 1
Where to Go? 4
What I Need 5
Timetable 6
When/Where to Start? 8
Room by Room Inventory/Disposition 11
Getting There... It's the little things that add up 22
    Planning ahead 24
    Estate and yard sales 24
    Auctions 25
    Consignments 26
    Donations 27
    Internet sales 28
    Photos and documents 29
    Clothes 29
    Food and household products 29
    Avoiding family feuds 30
    Appraisals 31
    Shredding 32
    Miscellaneous 32
Making the Move 33
    Moving day 34
    Last box 35
    After the move 35
    Dumpsters 36
    Pets 36
    Your new floor plan 36
    Say "NO" to storage 37
    Universal design 37
    Tips after you've set the moving date 38
    Survival kit for move day 38
    Services checklist 39
    Moving suggestions 40
Resources 41
Definitions 44
What to Look For 46
Evaluating Expenses 52
More Tips 53
National Association of Senior Move Managers 55
Moving for Seniors order form 56
Your New Floor Plan graph paper 58
Business Start-Up Opportunities 59

HOUSEHOLD DOWNSIZING

Introduction

Change isn't something most of us take lightly. Our lives have been one change after another. Most of us feel comfortable in our surroundings and dread the thought of ever giving up our homes. Yet, sometimes our homes become more than we can handle.

The house where our children were raised, although it holds so many memories, may become more than we can or want to take care of. Keeping up with both inside and outside maintenance and repairs can sometimes seem beyond our control. **But how do we start to make a change to smaller quarters?**

This workbook will help you and your family decide if it is time for a move, how to find a new home, how to make that move and much more. The questions may seem too simple in some cases, but these are sometimes the most difficult to answer. Once you decide you want to make a move, this workbook provides a step-by-step process you can use and lists of resources you and your family will find invaluable.

And if you don't want to move but have to, this workbook should make it easier for you and all concerned.

THIS END UP

Why move?

Sometimes outside forces tell us "it's time"— our health, our children, the too-big house, our ability to stay alone. Some questions to ask are, "Do I really want to stay here as long as I can? What would I need to stay: someone to cook, clean, take care of financial records, or yard help?" The list goes on.

If you and your family disagree on the need for you to move, there are outside (neutral) sources who can help you evaluate the situation. The resources section at the end of this workbook suggests places to call. Social workers, geriatric care maagers, discharge planners in hospitals, ministers, counselors, and physicians are among the people who can help you assess your living situation. Or they can help determine what modifications should be made (like having meals brought in, laundry sent out, etc.) for you to stay where you are.

The following questions may help you evaluate your particular situation concerning a move. Answer each one for yourself, then ask family members how they would respond to the questions about you. Note any other issues that are important to you.

1. Do I need someone to assist with personal tasks?
   (dressing, bathing, medications, walking, etc.) ❏ Yes ❏ No ❏ Sometimes

2. Do I need someone to prepare meals?
   (at least one well-balanced meal a day) ❏ Yes ❏ No ❏ Sometimes

3. Can I handle routine bills and financial records? ❏ Yes ❏ No ❏ Sometimes

4. Do I need someone with me overnight? ❏ Yes ❏ No ❏ Sometimes

5. Do I need someone to assist with:
   yard work? ❏ Yes ❏ No ❏ Sometimes

   laundry? ❏ Yes ❏ No ❏ Sometimes

   cleaning? ❏ Yes ❏ No ❏ Sometimes

   grocery shopping/errands? ❏ Yes ❏ No ❏ Sometimes

6. I need help with:
   _____
   _____
   _____

7. My family thinks I need help with:
   _____
   _____
   _____

MOVING TIP
Be sure to take pictures of each room before you start reorganizing/downsizing. You'll want to remember your home as it was before you started sorting everything getting ready to move.

You may want to make a move but your spouse/children see this as "their" home and want you to stay there forever. Perhaps they aren't aware that times change and you may not need as much space as you once did. Or you may know of major repairs needed for your house and don't want to go through that experience. Ask yourself and your spouse/children these questions:

> If you have a well-stocked pantry, try to deplete the supplies on hand. If you could outlast a nuclear blast with the canned soups you have, make an effort to 1) not purchase more, and 2) eat what you have. This also applies to the freezer. If you can't remember when you put it in, maybe you should throw it out.

1. Is this house is too big/old/etc. for me now?
   ❏ Yes ❏ No ❏ Maybe

2. Does it make sense to keep it when I don't use all this space most of the time?
   ❏ Yes ❏ No ❏ Maybe

3. Does it make sense for me to spend what it takes to keep this house going when I could live more simply somewhere else?
   ❏ Yes ❏ No ❏ Maybe

4. Do I feel isolated here?
   ❏ Yes ❏ No ❏ Sometimes

5. Can I ask my children, grandchildren and/or friends to visit more and to help with chores, etc?
   ❏ Yes ❏ No ❏ Maybe

6. The neighborhood isn't the same. Do I still feel safe here?
   ❏ Yes ❏ No ❏ Maybe

7. Are many of the services I need still close by? (doctor, grocery, neighbors, pharmacy, etc.)
   ❏ Yes ❏ No ❏ Maybe

8. Is this a good time to move? (season, to get family help, sell house, etc.)
   ❏ Yes ❏ No ❏ Maybe

9. What are some of the other reasons _to_ move?
   _____
   _____
   _____

10. What are some of the other reasons _not_ to move?
    _____
    _____
    _____

WHERE TO GO?

There are lots of factors to consider in deciding where you should go. What services do you need? How much can you afford? What is available in your community?

Should you stay in your current area or move closer to your children/family? Think about these questions and talk to your family and friends. When you are making a move, you need to project some of your needs for the future... not just next month. Planning ahead can eliminate additional moves down the road.

If your children or other family members are in other parts of the state/country, you might want to consider moving closer to them. (Keep in mind corporations are mobile today. If your children are moving every few years, this might not be the best idea for you.)

Downsizing can mean moving into a smaller house, condo, an apartment, a retirement community, a seniors' residence, a group home, an assisted living facility or other residence. Moving in with family members is another alternative. For an explanation of these terms, check the resource section on page 44. You and your family must decide what will work best for *you*.

Financing

If you are in a quandary about how to finance your move, use the **evaluating expenses chart** on page 52. There are many programs (federal, local and private) available to help you sort through the financial arrangements of selling a home and finding affordable housing. Many times the equity in your home can provide the funds for your retirement home. Reverse mortgages or renting your home are just two of the creative means to help you finance your move. Your accountant, attorney, tax preparer, financial planner, bank trust officer, or state social services agency are sources to help you find the answers. For the governmental agencies in your area, go to www.yourcity.gov or www.yourstate.gov. The main thing is don't be afraid to ask. This isn't something you do every day; you can't be expected to immediately know the best way to finance the choices you want. You worked hard for what you have now, so rely on the professionals to help you keep it.

Choosing a new home

As you look for a new place to live, consider some of these thoughts:
If you move to an apartment, house or condo, you may or may not have interaction with your neighbors or other people. You may feel somewhat isolated compared to living in your former neighborhood where you knew everyone and everyone knew you. Many seniors (especially widows and widowers) miss not seeing or talking with other people frequently and don't like eating alone. All retirement communities/facilities have personalities. Some are more formal than others. Some more "homey."

WHAT I NEED

1. Do I need a first floor (no steps) location?		❏ Yes	❏ No	❏ Maybe
2. Do I need a handicapped accessible place?		❏ Yes	❏ No	❏ Maybe
3. Do I need assistance with any daily living activities? (bathing, dressing, medications, toileting?)		❏ Yes	❏ No	❏ Maybe
4. Do I need at least *some* meals provided?		❏ Yes	❏ No	❏ Maybe
5. Do I need a place for my car?		❏ Yes	❏ No	❏ Maybe
6. Do I need something on a bus line or with transportation provided?		❏ Yes	❏ No	❏ Maybe
7. Do I need a place that will accept pets?		❏ Yes	❏ No	❏ Maybe
8. Do I need something near:	grocery	❏ Yes	❏ No	❏ Maybe
	pharmacy	❏ Yes	❏ No	❏ Maybe
	church	❏ Yes	❏ No	❏ Maybe
	doctor	❏ Yes	❏ No	❏ Maybe
	employment	❏ Yes	❏ No	❏ Maybe
	therapy	❏ Yes	❏ No	❏ Maybe
	bank	❏ Yes	❏ No	❏ Maybe
	other:			
9. Do I want someplace that offers some social activities?		❏ Yes	❏ No	❏ Maybe
10. Do I want a place with minimal maintenance/upkeep?		❏ Yes	❏ No	❏ Maybe
11. Do I want a place with a yard, patio, porch, etc.?		❏ Yes	❏ No	❏ Maybe
12. Do I want to:	own?	❏ Yes	❏ No	❏ Maybe
	rent?	❏ Yes	❏ No	❏ Maybe
	partially own?	❏ Yes	❏ No	❏ Maybe
13. Would adult day care provide the daytime assistance I need?		❏ Yes	❏ No	❏ Maybe

14. What other factors should I consider in looking for a new home?

TIMETABLE

The best case scenario is to move when you *want* to, on your timetable, not when you *have* to. One widow, while evaluating a retirement community, said that she wanted to move while she was still "in-charge." That way she could help direct where she would go, as well as what she would take with her and decide how to best dispose of the rest. But we don't always have the luxury of time; in fact, some people "wait too long" to make that move and are no longer physically or mentally able. When you move on *your* terms, you not only can be a part of the process, but have an easier adjustment to your new home. You have a chance to become involved with your new community at whatever level you wish.

If you can look at your situation now and decide that in two months, six months, or a certain month next year you want to make a move, write that down as your goal. **It will take all the effort you can muster to make that happen.** It isn't easy. But as with most things, once you decide to do it, a big part of the pressure is off. It just becomes how to do it. Fill out this questionnaire to get an idea what you are facing.

1. ❏ Male   ❏ Female

2. ❏ Single   ❏ Married   ❏ Widow/er
   If you have a spouse,
   how does she/he   ❏ agrees with   ❏ disagrees with
   feel about your downsizing?   ❏ no opinion   ❏ haven't discussed

3. Age range: ❏ 50–59   ❏ 60–69   ❏ 70–79
                            ❏ 80–89   ❏ 90 or over

4. Physical condition: ❏ excellent   ❏ pretty good for my age
                        ❏ seen better days   ❏ heading downhill

5. Mental conditon: ❏ excellent
                     ❏ pretty good for my age
                     ❏ many "senior moments"
                     ❏ losing ground fast

6. Children?   ❏ yes   ❏ no
   In this area? ❏ yes   ❏ no
   How many? _____ sons   _____ daughters

7. If you have children, how do they feel about your downsizing?
   ❏ agree with ❏ disagree with ❏ no opinion ❏ haven't discussed

8. Other family: ❏ yes ❏ no
   In this area? ❏ yes ❏ no
   How do they feel about your downsizing?
   ❏ agree with ❏ disagree with ❏ no opinion ❏ haven't discussed

9. Do you live in a: ❏ house? ❏ condo? ❏ apartment? ❏ other

10. Do you: ❏ rent? ❏ own?

11. Length of time you have lived at this residence?
    ❏ 1–5 years ❏ 6–10 years ❏ 11–20 years ❏ more than 21 years

12. Have you recently moved/downsized? ❏ yes ❏ no

13. The idea to move was:
    ❏ mine
    ❏ my spouse's
    ❏ my children's
    ❏ other family member's
    ❏ medical/physical necessity
    ❏ other

14. Would you like to move into smaller living quarters?
    ❏ yes ❏ no ❏ maybe

15. What type of home would you like to have?
    ❏ apartment ❏ condo ❏ smaller house
    ❏ seniors community ❏ share with another senior
    ❏ other

16. Can I count on spouse/children/other relatives to help with move?
    ❏ yes ❏ no ❏ maybe

17. I want to move: month_____ year_____

18. I want to live in this area: neighborhood_____
    city_____ state_____

19. I will need help to make this move:
    ❏ yes ❏ no ❏ maybe

WHEN TO START?

*I*f you are toying with the idea of making a change, you can start today. You can think, sort, and talk about it. What else? After you have answered the questions on page 5, talk to your friends who have already made a move. Do they like where they are? What do they like best, least? Would they move there again if they could do it over? Are they the types of people who won't be happy *anywhere*? Weigh the opinions you get from others, but also weigh the information you get from the admissions/rental people.

Every facility has a personality. Take time to visit, have a meal in the dining room, and spend the night (if possible before you sign on the dotted line). Some places have "respite" or guest rooms you can use for a night or two. Talk to residents to get their views. See the list on page 46 to help you evaluate and keep track of your visits.

Look at some of the apartments/rooms and check out the closet space, distance from the dining room, laundry area, etc.

Watch for ads in the newspaper or check the phone book for places that have the services you need/want. Schedule a visit and find out as much about them as possible. Eat a meal in the dining room; check out the various living arrangements. Use the chart on page 46 and compare prices/services.

Does the place you want have vacancies or must you put your name on a waiting list? This will give you some idea how long you have to get things in order for a move. Do you need to put a deposit down to hold the space you want? Is it refundable?

It might take you three to four months to sort things out and get ready for a move. With help, you might be able to do it faster, but you want to start as soon as possible—even if you don't have a move date established.

WHERE TO START?

*O*nce you have established you are going to move, you have crossed the biggest hurdle. The second thing is to decide *when*. Availability can be an issue and factors such as selling your home and coordinating family assistance for your move are other things to consider. It isn't going to be easy. But you have to start somewhere, sometime. Why not now?

If the whole prospect of moving seems overwhelming, you might want to consider contacting a Senior Move Manager. These individuals help with all aspects of the move. They may help you decide what to move, sort, pack, make all the moving arrangements, coordinate move day, unpack and help dispose of leftover items in the home by shipping, selling, or donating. Some Senior Move

Managers provide consulting services when you and/or your family members want to do some of the work. You can find a Smooth Transitions® Senior Move Manager by calling (502) 897-9332, or online at www.movingforseniors.com. Or contact the **National Association of Senior Move Managers** (NASMM) at www.nasmm.com. NASMM is a non-profit professional association of organizations dedicated to helping older adults and their families with the physical and emotional aspects of moving. Members are committed to maximizing the dignity and autonomy of older adults as they transition from one living environment to another.

Involve spouse, children and family as much as possible.

Use the inventory list beginning on page 11 to determine what items you will take to your new home, what family members will want and what needs to be disposed of. It helps if you know where you are going and what space you will have. But even if you aren't that far along in your planning, you know that some things will have to go. The sooner you identify those items and whether your family will take them or you will need to find new homes for them, the better.

If this seems like too much of a job, just do one room at a time.
This will give you time to digest the inventory you have and think about what you want to do with it.

You might want to take photos, videos, CDs or DVDs of items that you want family members to take.
If you don't have a digital camera, you can ask for your roll of film to be processed in CD form as well as prints so you can send to family members for viewing on their computer. If you take measurements of extra large pieces, it will also help them decide if they have room for the piece and what it will require to move it.

If you want to designate items for specific family and friends, use removable dots or sticky notes to identify items. . . select a color for individuals or use a number system.

For example, use a green note to identify the items you want to move to your new home. Use another color for things that are to be sold or donated, and yet another color for items going to specific family members. (Or "M" for move, "S" for sell, etc.) **The trick is to write down what the different colors mean**. This is especially important when others are helping and on the actual day of your move.

When you use sticky notes, you will find one of the best things about them is that they let you change your mind! What you decide to sell one day might be a treasure you want to take to your new home the next. Move the notes all you want now, for eventually you will have to **stick** with your decision.

If there are several children/family members involved, you may want to

·9·

write letters or initials on the sticky notes to indicate individuals to receive certain items. (J is for John, C is for Carol, etc.)

Before you move anything, take photos, videos, CDs or DVDs of each room as it is, from several angles. This will be a pleasant way for you and family members to remember each room before it becomes disheveled with the move. Exterior shots are also a good idea. You may want to "pan" general neighborhood shots as well.

If you have a floor plan of your new home, you will have a better idea of how much/which furniture you can actually take. Measure your furniture and see where it will fit in your new place. Will a couch be too big? Would a love seat work better? If you have oversized furniture, be sure to measure heights of pieces and ceilings in your new home. (Graph paper and cut-out furniture is on page 58.)

Be sure to measure under windows in case a piece of furniture might fit there. Make notes locating electrical outlets, phone jacks, cable hook-up, emergency call button and other things that will influence the placement of your things.

After you have measured your new space and your furniture, don't be lured into a false sense of "it will fit." Even if your new living room is only a foot shorter than your living room now, it doesn't mean all of the same things will fit. Is there room in the bedroom for the chest of drawers and both bedside tables? Will my kitchen table fit? Where will my television and favorite chair go? Is there enough room for my dining room table, buffet, china cabinet. . . all or some? Will the color schemes that I currently use look nice in my new surroundings?

> **Downsizing tip:**
> When you bring something new into the house, pitch something. . . from eyeglasses, electronics, towels, rugs, knick-knacks, you know the stuff. In fact, if you can get rid of two things, so much the better.

Will some of your meals be provided at your new home? If so, you won't need as much of your kitchen equipment, sets of dishes, pots and pans, baking things. Will someone else get to cook the Thanksgiving turkey ? Then you won't need the big roaster, service for twelve, linens and all the related items for the holiday feast.

Just because you think you will have room for furniture and things, the main question to ask is, "Do I use this, do I love it, do I have room for it?" When in doubt, don't move something to overcrowd your new home.

We all have so much. Sometimes we have become the repository for accumulations from past generations. Or your home is where those items that no one wants, but "we don't want them to get out of the family" reside.

If your home contains items from your children's high school and college experiences, let them know you are moving. Give them a date when those items must be gone or you will dispose of them You may have toys your grandchildren used and now they are grown.

ROOM BY ROOM INVENTORY/DISPOSITION

Bedroom 1

Item	Description/Measurements	Keep	Family*	Sell	Dispose
bed					
mattress	❏ single ❏ double ❏ queen ❏ king				
chest of drawers					
night stand(s)					
blanket chest					
chair(s)					
lamp(s)					
rug(s)					
television/radio					
pictures/wall hangings					
other					

* If you know which family member is to have a specific item, write their name/initials here

Bedroom 2

Item	Description/Measurements	Keep	Family*	Sell	Dispose
bed					
mattress	❏ single ❏ double ❏ queen ❏ king				
chest of drawers					
night stand(s)					
blanket chest					
chair(s)					
lamp(s)					
rug(s)					
television/radio					
pictures/wall hangings					
other					

* If you know which family member is to have a specific item, write their name/initials here

Bedroom 3

Item	Description/Measurements	Keep	Family*	Sell	Dispose
bed					
mattress	❏ single ❏ double ❏ queen ❏ king				
chest of drawers					
night stand(s)					
blanket chest					
chair(s)					
lamp(s)					
rug(s)					
television/radio					
pictures/wall hangings					
other					

Living Room

Book tip: Do you get Reader's Digest® Condensed Books? Are you a member of a book of the month club? When you are finished with them, pass them along to another reader. They are a little more difficult to get rid of in quantities. And others will want to read the selections while they are still popular.

Item	Description/Measurements	Keep	Family*	Sell	Dispose
couch	length style/color/fabric				
love seat					
end table(s)					
coffee table					
chair(s)					
secretary					
lamp(s)					
rug(s)					
stereo/audio equipment					
television					
pictures/wall hangings					
other					

* If you know which family member is to have a specific item, write their name/initials here

Dining Room

Item	Description/Measurements	Keep	Family*	Sell	Dispose
table	size _____ style/wood _____ extra leaves for table _____ table pads _____				
chair(s)	number _____				
buffet					
china cabinet					
tea cart					
china	pattern _____ number of place settings _____ serving pieces _____				
crystal/glassware	pattern _____ number of each style _____ silver _____				
flatware sterling	pattern _____ number of place settings _____				
silver plate	pattern _____ number of place settings _____				
mirror					
rug(s)					
pictures/wall hangings					
other					

·15·

Den

Item	Description/Measurements	Keep	Family*	Sell	Dispose
couch	length style/fabric				
love seat	length style/fabric				
chair(s)					
tables(s)					
lamp(s)					
rug(s)					
television/VCR/DVD					
stereo/audio equipment					
pictures/wall hangings					
other					

* If you know which family member is to have a specific item, write their name/initials here

Kitchen

Item	Description/Measurements	Keep	Family*	Sell	Dispose
stove	brand _____ age _____ ❏ gas ❏ electric				
refrigerator	brand _____ age _____				
table	size, style _____				
chairs	number _____				
microwave	brand _____ age _____				
small appliances					
dishes	pattern _____ place settings _____ serving pieces _____				
flatware	pattern _____ place settings _____ serving pieces _____				
cookware					
linens					
rug(s)					
pictures/wall hangings					
food items					
other					

Basement

Item	Description/Measurements	Keep	Family*	Sell	Dispose
washer	brand _____ age _____ ❏ gas ❏ electric				
dryer	brand _____ age _____ ❏ gas ❏ electric				
exercise equipment	brand _____				
sewing machine	brand _____				
pool table					
furniture (list)					
tools (list)					
other					

* If you know which family member is to have a specific item, write their name/initials here

Attic

Item	Description/Measurements	Keep	Family*	Sell	Dispose
furniture (list)					
other (list)					

Look in your underwear, sock and nightwear drawer. Now pick out those gowns/pajamas that you have been saving for "good." Start tonight and wear something new. And place that well-worn favorite in the rag bag. Those comfortable undies with the elastic just about shot... pitch' em. (One man who recently downsized had 70 pairs of socks in one drawer—not the socks he currently wore, just old socks he refused to throw away!)

Downsizing tip:
This is a test: How many plastic butter tubs do you have? How many empty Cool Whip® containers? Frozen dinner trays? Now, how many do you use in a week's time? Take the first number, subtract the second and pitch the rest. That wasn't hard was it? It is a significant first step in downsizing your life.

Garage

Item	Description/Measurements	Keep	Family*	Sell	Dispose
car(s)	model _____ style _____ year _____				
tools (list)					
lawn mower	brand _____ age _____				
other (list)					

* If you know which family member is to have a specific item, write their name/initials here

Miscellaneous

Item	Description/Measurements	Keep	Family*	Sell	Dispose
linens					
books					
computer/printer					
records/tapes/CDs					
video tapes					
collectibles					
plants					
holiday decorations					
piano/organ					
patio/yard furniture					
photo albums					
radios					
clothes					
shoes					
hats					
jewelry					
small electrical					
telephone(s)					
camera					
video camera					
other					

GETTING THERE...
IT'S THE LITTLE THINGS THAT ADD UP

While you're watching your favorite television program, especially if it is a rerun, take a drawer with you and a large garbage bag. Go through the items in that drawer and discard items you no longer need. Separate things that you will want to take with you from those items that need new homes.

If you keep plodding away at it a little at a time, you will be surprised at how much easier it will seem when move time finally comes. Even if your move won't be for another year or so, this process works for simplifying your life now.

Start now going through things in your closets, attic, basement, storage area and garage—not all at once, but a little at a time. Stay in one area, handle things one time and try to decide if it is something you use, love, someone in the family might want, need, or you can do without.

Take a tape recorder. Make notes of things you want to move, others to take, items to donate. It will help to keep all these thoughts/notes about your move and downsizing in one place.

Remember, you don't want to start over every time you go into a room. You want to handle things one time, stay in one room and stay focused.

You may also take snapshots of room areas or knick-knack shelves and identify items on the back. That small vase that doesn't look like much to others may be a special treasure from your childhood, travels, work life or activities. Even children who have been surrounded by those pieces all of their lives may not know (or appreciate) the stories behind them. If you don't let someone know, those treasures may be on the dust heap before you know it. Heirlooms need to be noted for their origin: side of the family, dates, how acquired and any other data you can provide. If you aren't able to do the documentation, ask someone to help you. This could be one of the most valuable projects you can undertake.

Even if your move isn't for a long time, the project will be much easier and less stressful, if you start today and keep at it. Think about all the things that are lurking around your house that you haven't used or needed for years. Let's get rid of the clutter before it is necessary to make a move.

If you have treasures—letters, pictures, mementos, you might want to combine them into a "memory box." It will be an easy way for you to store and revisit items that are special to you.

If space will be limited where you are going, remember that passing along furniture, pictures, and other treasures to your family gives you another reason to visit them. . . to see your things in new surroundings. It will also be a way for your children to have a piece of their childhood home in their adult home.

Remember, if you give furniture to children you can visit it, but you don't have to dust it! But don't be disappointed if your children don't want your furniture. They may have a house full of their own things and no room for your treasures. Some adult children are moving around in their jobs and don't want more things to move or they have different decorating styles. The Victorian loveseat you cherish just won't fit in with the contemporary look your son has in his apartment.

If you have a gallery of photos on your walls and won't have the same space in your new home, put those treasured photos in album(s). You can look at them whenever you like. As you reorganize, divide photos by families, so one day you can pass them along to those individuals.

If you have lots of pictures of family and/or travels and limited space, here are a few suggestions. Select some special shots and combine them into one or more album(s). Another idea is to convert your photos/slides to video tape, CD, or DVD. There are companies that will help you with this. Look in the Yellow Pages or online under video tape duplication and transfer.

If you have a collection of items (such as figurines), consider taking only a few representatives as a reminder, without the space requirements of the whole collection.

Remember the tip to mark items from your inventory list with sticky notes, removable dots or color code things that will be going with you, items family members are going to take, items that will be sold or donated, or trashed. By using sticky notes or removable dots, you are able to change your mind and move them around. But this process is essential to getting the project started.

Items family members want can be the most frustrating. They may want these things, but they don't want to commit to coming to get them or arranging for shipment. It may be necessary to give your family deadlines for getting items out. If they can't pick them up, there are other ways to handle the situation. Movers, bus lines, and various shipping, packing and mailing places can help you here. Parcel post is often cheaper than professional movers. Professional movers may have minimum poundage requirements for a move. There are also companies that specialize in small shipments and/or places who will ship individual pieces of furniture. (See list of resources.)

MOVING TIP
Have you collected those little soaps and shampoos and sewing kits on your travels? Either use them, or better still, donate them to a homeless shelter.

Planning ahead

*I*n your new home make note of where electrical outlets are. This will help when placing furniture. You may need a power strip to use for multiple items like a bedside lamp, radio, clock, electric blanket, phone, and others. It is easier to have one of those strips handy as the movers are putting the bed together so you can have access to the wall before the furniture gets in place. Make note of where the cable TV hook-up is so you can arrange your furniture in a comfortable setting.

Measure the length, height, and depth of the closet space in your new home. Now, measure what you have in your present home. If it is easier for you to visualize the amount of space you will have in your new closet, you might want to put tape down on the floor to the dimensions of your new closet(s).

Simple arithmetic will tell you that you must eliminate some (many!) clothes, linens, coats, cleaning, and pantry items. Don't just expect to "transfer" things from one closet to another.

For increased closet space, consider adding a double rack in your new place. This would allow blouses/shirts and lightweight items to hang above skirts, pants and other short things. One section can be left for long, dress-length things and robes. Most large home improvement stores, hardware and discount stores carry closet supplies and materials. There are also companies who will do this for you. Check the Yellow Pages/online under "closet design/remodeling or organizers. In some cases the facility you are moving to will offer some assistance with this free or for a

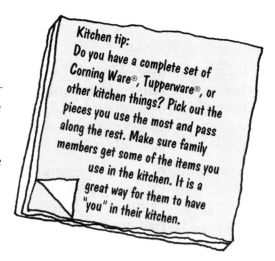

Kitchen tip:
Do you have a complete set of Corning Ware®, Tupperware®, or other kitchen things? Pick out the pieces you use the most and pass along the rest. Make sure family members get some of the items you use in the kitchen. It is a great way for them to have "you" in their kitchen.

nominal charge. Start with them before you line up an entire system from an outside vendor.

Estate and yard sales

*B*e careful what you throw away. Items you consider very ordinary may have some value to a collector. . . and we are not just talking about antiques. Almost anything is collected these days. . . from reamers and baseball cards to pottery and even those ladies head vases we loved years ago. So while you may not want something and your family has no interest, have a reliable person give you an assessment of your belongings before you just chuck them out the door. Some of your smaller items may bring more than large furniture pieces.

A yard sale is one way to dispose of items you no longer want. But keep in mind they take a lot of work and the right location and may not generate the money you hoped. There are services that will conduct a house/yard or "estate" sale for you. They are listed in the telephone book under estate/tag sales. They are experts on pricing and marketing and can increase the amount of money you might generate by doing it yourself. Ask how they charge, what percentage commission, other fees, etc., before you sign up. Make sure it fits with the timing you have for being out of the house. Some neighborhoods have restrictions on estate/yard sales. Check to see if sales are allowed in your neighborhood. If you want to have an estate sale after you move, include this in your real estate agreement.

Some neighborhood, church and community groups have sales, where, generally for a small fee, you are allowed to bring your items to a local site and sell your things there. Check to see if you get to keep the proceeds or they go to the sponsoring organization.

> **Downsizing tip:**
> Whenever the DAV, Amvets, or other organization calls and says a truck will be on your street on a given day, and asks if you have anything to donate, say "<u>yes</u>." The week or so lead time will give you enough warning and enough motivation to sort through some things. Every bagful of things you can donate before you move will be items you won't have to worry about where they should go.

Auctions

Another way to make money from some of your belongings is to auction them. The auction can be at your home, or the auction house will take your belongings to their location for sale. Generally, the auction people will evaluate the items you have for sale and either offer you money on the spot, or they will auction the items off to the highest bidder and keep a percentage of the gross sales. (This can run from 20–30 percent of total, plus a fee for picking up large items.) Most auctioneers will tell you that the same five items on sale at five auctions in a row can bring five different prices because different people attend, looking for different things.

Check the classifieds in your local newspaper, generally Sunday editions, and you will find a list of the upcoming auctions in your area. This will give you a feel for the types of items sold. Various items run in cycles —what is in demand today may not be worth as much next month/year. Items that may not bring big prices at auction now may be the hot new collectible next year. Electronics (TV, recorders, etc.) return very little in relation to their cost due to changing technology. And because trends in home furnishings and colors change, that practically new sofa you have might not bring as much as you hoped.

To find an auction company in your area, check the Yellow Pages under auctions, estate sales, or look online under www.auctionzip.com.

If you own genuine antiques you want to sell, you should have your items appraised by a professional. Even if you are selling them individually to family and friends, you may want to know the current market value. Check the resource section on page 39.

You might want to consider selling big appliances (washer, dryer, refrigerator) by placing an ad in the local classifieds; and by all means, **tell everyone you know that you are going to be getting rid of things.** Young people setting up housekeeping, folks with summer cabins and college students furnishing apartments are always on the lookout for good items. Check the newspaper for ads to get a feel for how much to ask. Think about how long you have had the item and how much you paid for it in the first place. Appliances and electronics depreciate a lot and will not return as much as you might think.

Used record and book stores may be interested in your collections. Check the Yellow Pages or online for the dealers closest to you. Some book stores have "out-of-print" book specialists who might be looking for some of the books you have.

Be careful about placing an ad in the newspaper especially if you live alone, or in a questionable neighborhood. In most circumstances, selling to people you know or who have referred someone to you is probably safer than encouraging true strangers into your home.

> Are you saving aluminum pie tins? You never know when you might need one . . . but ten is too many. Save a couple and pitch or recycle the rest.

Don't forget ebay, Amazon, and other online places to sell your books.

If you have a collection of books on a special subject (art, gardening, sports, parapsychology, etc.), contact groups or organizations that deal in that subject. They could buy all or part of your collection; or you could donate the collection to share the resources with others who have the same interest. Some local organizations, including the library, may collect books and then sell them as a fund-raiser. (See the section on donations, page 27.)

Consignments

Many areas have consignment shops that will take your goods to sell and you will receive a percentage of the selling price. Check some of the shops, antique malls and such in your area to get an idea of the items they sell. Find out what percent they charge, how long they will keep your items and what happens if the items don't sell. Some shops specialize in specific goods, clothes, furniture, styles and items. Do as much work by phone as you can. Some shops will give you cash and provide pickup service. If this is important to you, ask.

Many shops take new items only on certain days and times. Call before you drop in unannounced with a carload of things. If you can, you might want to take a photo of what you have and email

> Pack rat tip:
> Do you have a hodgepodge collection of appliances, radios, phones, etc. that don't work as well as they used to. . . or not at all? Get rid of them. No, you won't need them for extra parts, you won't go back to them if your present item breaks down. Now, either put them in the trash, or if they might have some life in them, donate them to a group that might rehab them.

or take it to the consignment shop to see if they will take them, before you take the items themselves.

Again, ask what commission percentage they charge, how long they will keep an item, how/if they will price and reduce the price, what they do with the item if it doesn't sell, and how often they send a check for your payment.

Donations

*I*f you want to get rid of your belongings without selling them, you can donate them. There are a number of organizations that will come get your things. Some have drop-off centers. Think about organizations you support and find out if they take donations of furniture, clothing, household items, books, tools, etc. Some groups will take only certain items, and you might need to call more than one place. (A general list is in the resource section.)

Some libraries and/or schools have periodic used book sales. Watch for mention of them in the newspaper or call to find out if the one nearest you has such a sale. Ask what they will and will not take (hardback, paperback, magazines, *Reader's Digest® Condensed Books*, encyclopedias, *Book of the Month Club* books, children's, first editions). Do they pick up?

Some charitable institutions send used text books and educational volumes to other countries. Consider donating your book collection to them.

Collections of figurines, dolls, toys, etc. might be appreciated by children at a local hospital. They could be put on display for many children to view. What a perfect way to share what you have enjoyed all those years.

Old eyeglasses you find in drawers can be recycled. There are several groups/organizations, such as the Lions Club, some churches, ophthalmologists, optometrists, and funeral homes, that collect old contact lenses and eyeglasses. You may have old sunglasses, "wraparounds," readers, or lenses without frames that can be used again.

Hearing aids you no longer use can be refurbished and used again. Some local organizations like the March of Dimes collects them, or you can send them to *Hear Now* (see Resource Section, page 42).

If you have medical equipment/ supplies that are still usable but you no longer need, groups like Hospice would be glad to have them. Specific items related to diabetes can be used by the American Diabetes Association or other organizations in your community. Homeless centers are frequently in need of health/medical supplies (walkers, braces, bandages, prostheses, pads, crutches). If you have medical equipment (walkers, potty chairs, or other devises), they are much in demand by groups treating indigents. Make a few calls and find someore who can use those things you no longer need. Ask if they can pick up the items.

> Holiday tip:
> What about those holiday decorations? Do you have "good" ones you currently use and then those you've had forever that are a little shabby, out-of-date or maybe don't work anymore? See what you have and what you might use in your new place and pass along the rest. If it would make you feel better, hum a few holiday tunes as you do it!

Wigs and hair pieces you have but no longer want are welcomed by various groups serving cancer patients. Check your phone book for organizations providing these.

Nursing homes and adult day care centers welcome donations of puzzles, craft or hobby projects, including leftover tools or supplies.

When making your donations, be sure to ask for a receipt so you can deduct the amount from your taxes. The amounts may not seem like a lot at the time, but, as with many small things, they add up. This goes for items picked up as well as dropped off. Sometimes it is necessary to ask for a receipt; organizations may not automatically give one.

Internet sales

*I*f you have access to the internet, there are many ways to find out what various items are worth. You may even sell them on line. You can research things collectors are seeking on America Online through their classified and collectible areas. Other popular websites are eBay, (www.eBay.com), Amazon (amazon.com) and skybid (www.skybid.com), on-line auctions.

Do you have a coupon drawer and a place where you accumulate junk mail? File the coupons by expiration date (month) and pitch the out-of-date ones. Keep junk mail and catalogues from taking over. If you aren't able to keep up with it on a daily basis, set up a few minutes each week to sort through them... throw as much of it away as you can. How many pizza coupons does one person need anyway?

Through Yahoo, AOL, Google or other search engines, you can get comparative pricing on your items. Some provide names of collector clubs/organizations that can lead to additional information or outlets in your area (Avon bottle collectors, Beam bottle collectors, train memorabilia, to name a few).

For non-computer people, there are books/newsletters for collectibles available in libraries and bookstores. *Kovels' Antiques and Collectibles Price List* and *Shroeder's Antiques Price Guide* are two of the largest guidebook publishers in this field. There are many books devoted entirely to specific items. Your collection might be worth more than you realize, especially if you can find the right buyer!

Photos and documents

*I*f you have old photos, letters, or other documents in which you or no one in your family has great interest, this could be the perfect time to donate them to the local historical society, college or university. Do not throw them away just because you don't want them. They could provide insight into life at another time. **The same goes for old school yearbooks, financial records, your first paycheck, copies of hospital bills from the birth of your children, diplomas and wedding licenses. Find good homes for them.**

Old yearbooks are frequently needed by their respective schools to fill holes in their collections or as general archive material. Contact the administration or alumni office of the school; they might know a representative in your area who could pick up the book. (These books are generally heavy and you might not want to mail them, but don't let that stop you from trying to find someone who wants them.)

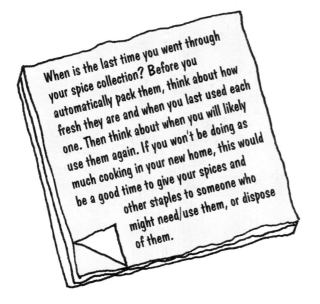

When is the last time you went through your spice collection? Before you automatically pack them, think about how fresh they are and when you last used each one. Then think about when you will likely use them again. If you won't be doing as much cooking in your new home, this would be a good time to give your spices and other staples to someone who might need/use them, or dispose of them.

Clothes

*M*any organizations will take used clothing. Consignment shops generally request items be clean and still have some wearability left in them. Other organizations might not be as picky. Call and check out your favorite charities to see if they have any requirements for donated clothing.

Certain vintage clothing is in demand. Check the telephone book for vintage clothing consignment shops that may be interested in your items. Call first; much of their work is done by appointment only.

Some school drama departments, local theatres and playhouses like to have vintage clothing to use in their productions. Call the school and ask the drama teacher to call you back. Describe what you have, see if there's an interest, and plan how you can get together.

Food and household products

*I*f you move to a place that provides meals, you may have excess food on hand that needs to get to folks who can use it. Check the phone book to find names of local food banks or check with your church office to see if they know of anyone who could use your pantry items.

You might consider an item out-of-date if it does not have a bar code on it, or a "sell or use by" date. Both of these features have been added to canned goods long enough now, that if yours doesn't have it, better dispose of it instead of moving or donating it.

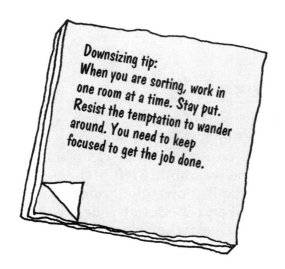

Downsizing tip:
When you are sorting, work in one room at a time. Stay put. Resist the temptation to wander around. You need to keep focused to get the job done.

If you have an estate sale, many times they will be able to sell the leftover soap powder, cleaning products, and food items you have. Ask before you dispose of these. (The auction staff might also be able to sell these things.)

The same applies for household cleaning supplies and yard paraphernalia if you are moving somewhere you won't need them. Some churches, camps, etc. appreciate having tools and yard equipment to maintain their property. Check it out.

Avoiding family feuds

You have accumulated a lifetime of treasures and want your children to have some of them, but perhaps you don't know how to make it happen without a referee.

Although you will be moving some of your treasures, this is a good time to determine where some of your things will go when you no longer have use for them. Here are a few techniques you can modify for your use.

Putting sticky notes or removable dots on items that **you** want specific children to have has already been mentioned. It also works for items your children have noted that **they** want. But what do you do when all want certain things? When the family is all together, you can issue them an **equal** amount of play money and let them "bid" on the items they most want. This gives them a chance to get something that has more meaning to them, regardless of their actual budget. (The bidding and buying process can be done on paper as well as with play money.)

If you have more than one child, another easy technique is to let them each pick an item, in turn from oldest child to youngest, then reverse the order and let the youngest pick first until the items you want them to have are all chosen. If you wish to keep track on dollar amounts individuals are receiving, you can "price" things ahead of time (again with sticky notes). When the choosing is done, tally the amount each child has and see what, if anything, needs to be done to equalize shares.

Some people put off moving because they don't want to deal with dividing things among children. Don't let this stand in the way of having a new home. It need not be a bloody battle. But don't be too disappointed if the things you value most are of little interest to your children. People's decorating styles and tastes in general are different. And what looks great in your house may not fit the lifestyle of your children. Another way of taking turns is to draw numbers so that the oldest and the youngest don't always get the first pick.

> Pack rat tip:
> Do you have a tendency to save the magazines you receive? When you have read them, pass them along. Either give them to a friend or to a local hospital, nursing home. If there are articles you want to keep for reference, tear them out, but keep the magazine moving. Try not to let them get backed up... others want them when they are still current.

Appraisals

With so many people watching *Antiques Roadshow* on television, it is easy to think you have some valuables among your belongings. Should you have your things appraised? The first question to ask yourself is *why*? If you are doing it for your own curiosity, consider that it will cost for this service. Appraisers generally charge hourly and according to the type of document you need. If the appraisal is for insurance purposes, then the values need to be on the high side. If they are for probate, and therefore for tax purposes, then you would want the values to be on the low side. When you are trying to make a division between children equitable, then they might be able to do something of a more informal nature. You might be having something appraised that you are going to ship or donate and need a valid evaluation.

Just because something is appraised for a certain value doesn't mean you will be able to sell it for that amount. Be sure to ask questions of the appraiser before you ask for their advice. How much does it cost, how long to get the report, what are their qualifications (areas of special expertise)? The person who does the appraisal should not be the person who might purchase it from you.

Appraisers can be found in the Yellow Pages/online. Many of the auction services also do appraisals. Courts use appraisers for probate and might be able to give you the names of some they would recommend.

Shredding

Not a day goes by without someone having his or her identity stolen. There are basic things to think about and do, even if you are not moving. Any paper in your home that you are going to get rid of that has any banking, financial, social security number or any personal information should be shredded.

When you put your tax return away for this year and dispose of the past year's, be sure to shred the old one before you trash it. Most professionals say you need to keep seven to ten years of tax records. Ask your tax preparer for a recommendation.

Old medical bills and records should also be shredded. When in doubt, shred it. New offers for credit cards and similar solicitations should be shredded as well.

If you have lots to shred, there are companies who can do this for you. You can either take it to them, or they will come to your home and shred it there. Check the Yellow Pages or online for this service.

Miscellaneous

When you move to smaller quarters, you will find you no longer need four sets of sheets for each bed. A set on the bed and a set on standby is enough. You don't need as many sets of bath towels either. Pick your favorites and those special ones you reserve for guests and use them.

You also won't use as many items such as kitchen towels, potholders, etc. You may stop cooking altogether and just need something to dry your hands and wipe up spills.

This is a good time to get rid of those big turkey roasters, serving platters and items you only use when the clan gathers.

If you have heirloom linens that you have used for holidays when the family gathers, consider offering them to whomever takes your dining suite. Some handmade linens, if they are in pristine condition, can be sold at auction, consignment, or estate sale.

Just how many sets of dishes will you really need? Will you still be doing a lot of cooking and entertaining? You may want to keep one set of dinnerware, but you may not need twelve place settings. This might be the time to start using that favorite set of china and crystal for everyday and getting as much pleasure as you can from it.

There will be vases, serving pieces, and all sorts of things you hadn't thought about in a long time. **Start labeling, sorting and making your lists right away, because that moving day will be here before you know it!** After reviewing these miscellaneous items, add the extras to your "sell" or "donation" stacks.

MAKING THE MOVE

*I*f you are in an apartment, you will need to give notice. If you have a house or condo to sell, contact a real estate agent. Ask your friends to recommend someone or look in the Yellow Pages and online. Check "for sale" signs in your neighborhood to see who knows your area and call them.

Once you make the decision to move and have another place lined up, the ball starts rolling. The Post Office provides a booklet that is very useful. It has mail forwarding information, change-of-address forms and a timetable of things that need to be done before your move.

Notify magazine subscriptions of your change of address as soon as you have a moving date. It sometimes takes publishers several months to adjust their records.

Put all of the information related to your move together in a binder, large brown envelope or folder. Keep it in a safe place. Be sure to ask if your mover offers a discount for seniors.

If the more you think about this move, the more you think a little help would be good, a Senior Move Manager (SMM) might be the answer to your prayers. They can provide the direction you need and do as much of the hands-on work as you want. From sorting through years of household items, personal papers, clothes, to packing/unpacking and making all the moving arrangements, they make it easy for you and your family. And when your family is spread all over the country or have job responsibilities that take a lot of their time, a SMM can fill in those key tasks in a professional and knowledgeable way. Check **www.movingforseniors.com** for a Smooth Transitions® office, or call 502-897-9332 or the National Association of Senior Move Managers, **www.NASMM.com**, to find help near you.

Contact a mover. Ask your friends/family for recommendations or check in the Yellow Pages or online. Ask the staff where you are moving if they have movers they would recommend. It is best to set this up at least a month in advance. Weekday moving usually costs less than weekends.

Movers are generally busier at the end of the month, so try to schedule your move for the beginning or middle of the month.

Try to be the first move of the day to give yourself more time to get unpacked. If possible, move early in the week to give the place where you are moving more time to follow-up on little things that might need to be done. Many facilities have fewer staff on the weekend to help with your "move-in" assistance. Moving earlier in the week will also allow more time for cable hookup, phone installation, deliveries, etc.

Movers can do the packing for you. They have the supplies and expertise. If they do the packing they can schedule it just before you move so you won't have to look at boxes for weeks ahead of the move. But this also requires your "sorting" skills to decide what you are actually going to move.

Ask if your mover will provide boxes ahead of time and/or pick up after your move. This could be a cost and time saving effort.

As you talk to movers and interview them about your move, find out if they have any special restrictions on items they won't/can't move (like plants, lamps, liquor, mirrors, glass tops, pictures). Are there extra charges involved for those items? Must your washer/dryer be unhooked for them to be moved? What about your computer, patio furniture, flammable items, gas grill?

It isn't always necessary to empty drawers of dressers and cabinets. But make sure anything that you leave in the drawers will not break. If you have small loose items, you might want to place them in plastic bags or otherwise secure them. Movers may turn furniture pieces on end to get them in and out of your home and things may shift.

Moving day

Are you counting on family and friends to help you move? Work with them on the schedule. Many of them will need to arrange to be off work or for child care.

If family members are taking some of your household items, make sure they know when they need to get those items before you move.

As you are scheduling your move, be sure to check with your new place to see if there are any restrictions on when/where/how you move in. Because of access to entrances, elevators, loading docks and related issues, some places only schedule one move per day within certain hours. Find out what the requirements are where you are moving.

Try to arrange good helpers so that you won't have to be there the day of the move. As long as you can have a trusted person to oversee the move-out and move-in, you are better off visiting a friend that day. Come back to your new home after things have settled a bit.

If the movers have been especially helpful, careful, and/or efficient, it is acceptable to tip them. Give the tip, ten to fifteen percent of the total, preferably in cash, to the team coordinator to divide among the workers.

You might want to have some soft drinks, water and/or snacks on moving day. The movers will take a break and, if they get your items loaded by lunchtime, they may stop on the way to your new place for a quick meal before they unload.

Last box

Have a "last box" ready to hold assorted small items on the day of move. Keys to the secretary/desk, the remote control, picture hangers, odd nail, bolts, screws, anything that seems leftover as you empty the house.

Be sure to carry your vital medicines with you so that they will not get misplaced or caught up with the other boxes.

If you feel more comfortable doing so, transport your most valuable jewelry yourself.

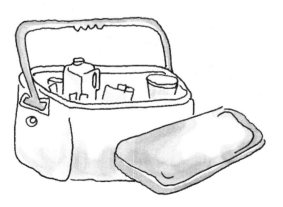

> How many screwdrivers, hammers, wrenches, and miscellaneous tools do you have? You might want to take a small tool box with you with pliers, hammer, screwdrivers, tape measure, etc. But you probably won't need the assortment you have now. Check for duplicates. Dispose of the extras.

Use a cooler for refrigerated/freezer items. Pack last, open first. If you have medicines that are refrigerated, put those in the cooler that is the last on the truck, and first off at your new place.

You want to get unpacked as quickly as possible and you might want to get extra help to do so. The day of the move the priorities are to make up the bed, and unpack the bathroom and kitchen, in that order. The more you can get unpacked with extra hands, the better. It is unsettling to face boxes that need unpacking day after day.

After the move

Once you have moved to your new home, if there are items left at the old place, call and arrange to have those items donated, sold, or hauled away. If a general cleaning of the old place is required, get a cleaning service to do this for you. It will be well worth the money.

Be sure to find out the restrictions for disposing of hazardous material that you might have stored in your home/garage (paint, antifreeze, cleaning supplies, mineral spirits, old computers, electronics, yard chemicals, etc.).

Dumpsters

If your family thinks the best solution for the leftovers of your move is to get a dumpster, it might be easy, but not necessarily smart. Many of your treasures have value to others either monetarily or as an item that is still useable. Yes, it takes time, but some insignifant items might be just the thing some collector wants. Better safe than sorry when disposing in haste.

There may be restrictions in your neighborhood about dumpsters. Be sure to check this out before you order one.

Pets

If animals are part of your life, finding a place to move where you can take your four-legged, or feathered friend is important. Many facilities allow pets. Look for one that does. If you have an assortment of pet toys, leashes, feeding/water bowls, bedding and related items from past pets, there are several organizations that welcome those things. Animal shelters are even happy to get those towels, blankets and sheets that may not be suitable for people.

Your new floor plan

As you arrange furniture in your new home, keep safety features in mind. Clear pathways, eliminate loose rugs, ensure proper lighting and place items in cabinets within safe reach.

If the new place where you are moving doesn't have a floor plan for you to use, you can make your own. (See graph paper and cut-out furniture on page 58.) If you want to enlarge this page, take to a copy/print shop in your neighborhood. Be sure to increase the furniture pieces too.

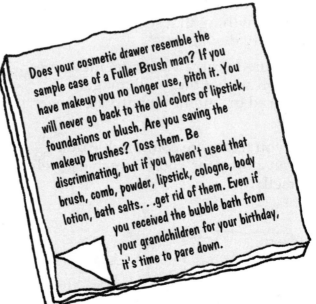

Does your cosmetic drawer resemble the sample case of a Fuller Brush man? If you have makeup you no longer use, pitch it. You will never go back to the old colors of lipstick, foundations or blush. Are you saving the makeup brushes? Toss them. Be discriminating, but if you haven't used that brush, comb, powder, lipstick, cologne, body lotion, bath salts. . .get rid of them. Even if you received the bubble bath from your grandchildren for your birthday, it's time to pare down.

Say "NO" to storage

As tempting as it may seem to rent a storage place in which to put those "leftover" items and things you just don't want to decide on right now, **DON'T**. There are several reasons *not* to store.

- Things you store frequently aren't worth the monthly fees you will pay for keeping them.
- The longer items are left in storage, the less likely you will even remember what they are and why you kept them in the first place.
- And you don't need the thought of "that storage place" hanging over your head.

Universal design

After reading this workbook, there may be some of you who think you would rather stay where you are than move. You may want to consider "universal design" as a way to do it. This means barrier-free or accessible design to provide a level of accessibility —not only for persons with disabilities —but for everyone. It might mean ramps instead of stairs, wider light switches, lever handles for doors instead of knobs, wider interior doors, pull-out shelves, etc.

For some who don't want to move, finding a professional to make the appropriate modifications in the home might be a solution. Certainly looking at places to move with universal design will help you to stay there longer. Check medical supply/equipment businesses for names of companies to do your modifications.

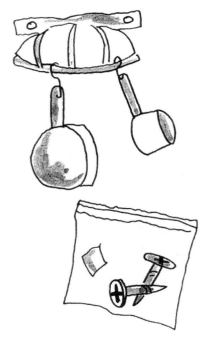

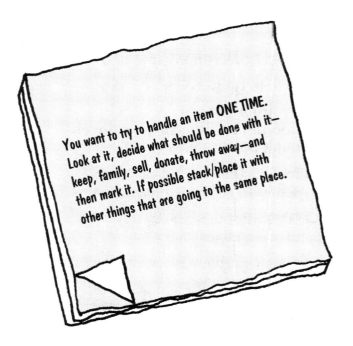

You want to try to handle an item ONE TIME. Look at it, decide what should be done with it— keep, family, sell, donate, throw away—and then mark it. If possible stack/place it with other things that are going to the same place.

Tips after you've set the moving date

Once you know where (and when) you are going, have pre-printed address labels made. Some "quick printers" can make labels for you while you wait. These will make it easier to let people know your new address.

Make a list of your physicians, dentist, friends, bank, hair dresser, church office, attorney, accountant, credit card companies and others to let them know you're making a move. Tell them the effective date and give them your new address and phone number, if possible. The post office has change-of-address forms you may use.

If you are moving away from your neighborhood, be sure to get copies of your personal records to use with your new doctors, lawyers and other providers. Ask them for referrals where possible.

When you send your holiday greetings next year, do yours early so friends with whom you have only yearly contact will have your new address before they send their cards. Depending on the time of year, you might want to send a "I have a new address" notice to friends and relatives.

Some moving companies have counselors who can work with you, offering many suggestions/tips on making a successful move. You might want to consider using a Senior Move Manager to help with move day.

Have a survival kit for day of the move

- ❏ keys to new home
- ❏ medicines
- ❏ bottled water
- ❏ checkbook (to pay movers)
- ❏ cash to tip movers
- ❏ bathroom basics (toothbrush/toothpaste, towel, toilet paper, soap)
- ❏ tool kit (hammer, nails, tape, screwdriver, tape measure,)
- ❏ box cutter or scissors to open boxes
- ❏ plastic garbage bags
- ❏ lightbulbs
- ❏ kitchen basics (paper towels, plates, plastic utensils, cups,)
- ❏ cleaning basics (sponge, cleansers, liquid soap, dust rag, etc.)
- ❏ pen/pencil/marker
- ❏ clock
- ❏ flashlight
- ❏ extra eyeglasses
- ❏ address book
- ❏ telephone
- ❏ change of clothes
- ❏ other (list) _____
_____
_____
_____
_____

Services checklist

*L*eaving where you are means notifying these people of your pending move. For some you will be transferring services, for others cancelling.

Service	Date to end/change service	Date completed
gas/electric*		
water*		
phone		
long distance carrier		
cable		
insurance coverage**		
mail service/Post Office		
yard service		
snow removal		
trash removal		
laundry service		
newspaper carrier		
house cleaning		
security system		
voter registration		

* utilities generally left on until house is sold and transferred to new owner at that time

** switch to renter's insurance

Photo tip:
Your family photo wall can be condensed into a photo album if you won't have the wall space in your new home. Be sure to write on the back the identity of the individuals in the photos and a year/date if possible.

Moving suggestions

*I*f you are planning to do a lot of the move yourself, here are some other suggestions that might be useful:

- You can get good boxes (new or used) from truck rental companies and movers.

- Use more medium sized boxes than large ones (easier to move, fill, unpack).

- Use towels and other linens you are going to take as packing material.

- Truck rental businesses and movers have "wrapping paper" (unprinted newspaper). This is good for packing dishes and other items and is much cleaner than newspaper.

- For very fragile items, use bubble wrap and packing peanuts. Gift shops might save a plastic bag of these for you, or check with local mailing companies. Some truck rental companies and movers also have these.

- Use extra tape on the bottom of boxes to reinforce them.

- Pack like items together (heavy items in small boxes, lighter items in larger boxes).

- Mark boxes with numbers and indicate rooms where they go.

- Keep a master list of the boxes and their contents, as well as to which room they belong.

- Indicate with markers boxes that contain "fragile" items.

- Use zip top plastic bags to hold small items (parts of a lamp, for example, then tape to the lamp).

- Have tape, scissors, and markers ready as you pack and unpack.

- Pack one or two boxes and mark "pack last/open first." It would have bed linens, bath items, clothes for the first few days, coffee pot/coffee mugs, pan, one or two place settings of flatware and dishes, flashlight, radio, clock, remote control, snacks, etc. This should hold you over till you get all your boxes unpacked.

- Put checklists and inventories on clipboards. Stay near the door and check inventory as boxes are loaded and unloaded. This might be a good job for a family member or eager friend.

- On moving day, park your car and those of helpers out of the garage, off the driveway, and out of the way of the movers.

- You want to try to handle an item ONE TIME. Look at it, decide what should be done with it—keep, family, sell, donate, throw away—and then mark it. If possible stack/place it with other things that are going to the same place.

- Be sure to leave the garage door opener at your home for new tenants.

- Leave appliance instructions and warranties , furnace, air conditioning, security system info, roof, irrigation, neighborhood association rules/contacts, condo directives or any other things that are significant to the new owners. A kitchen drawer or cabinet is a good place to leave these. Same for keys, openers, or other items important for the house. Your realtor may take charge of this; but if not, you can.

RESOURCES

Services provided in each community are different. The same services may have different names or titles. **By looking in the telephone directory or online under some of these headings, you should be able to find the types of services available in your area.** Some of the headings will give you alternate places to find similar listings. You might need to be a little creative in coming up with the listings you need, but as they say, "let your fingers do the walking" for you.

Looking for a place to live:

Apartments

Assisted living

Condominiums

Geriatric care managers

Geriatric consulting services

Human services organizations

Local government (services for seniors)

Marriage, family, individual counselors

National Association of Senior Move Managers, www.NASMM.com, 877-606-2766

Nursing homes

Nursing homes referral service

Real estate agents

Relocation services

Retirement & life carecommunities & homes

Senior citizens' services

Senior Housing Locator www.SNAPforSeniors.com

Senior residences

Social service organizations

Social workers

Your local government.gov

If you need assistance to stay where you are:

Day care centers–adult

Geriatric consulting services

Home health organizations

Hospital–discharge planners

House cleaning services

Human service organizations

Maintenance services

Marriage, family, individual counselors

Meal delivery services/ Meals on Wheels

Rehabilitation services

Senior citizens' services

Sitting services

Social service organizations

Social workers

Transportation

Yard/lawn services

When you decide to move:

Movers (residential)

Moving services–labor & material

Moving supplies

National Association of Senior Move Managers, www.NASMM.com, 877-606-2766

Packaging services

Pianos & organ moving

Shipping–packages, supplies

Shredding

Smooth Transitions
www.movingforseniors.com
502-897-9332

Truck rental

Unpacking services

What to do with your treasures:

(places to look if you want to sell or donate items)

Antique dealers

Appraisals

Auctions

Books/records/tapes (sell/donate)
 used book/record/tape places
 libraries, schools, civic clubs, church groups, books on specific subjects to organizations interested in same (gardening, trains, etc.)

Books–used & rare

Collectibles

Collections (donate)
 children's hospital (for example: collection of rabbit figurines)
 school (collection of wildlife magazines)
 museum (collection of civil war memorabilia)
 historical home/site (antique linens/items)

Consignment services

Craft supplies (donate to)
 nursing homes
 day care centers
 adult day care centers
 nursery schools
 church schools

Ebay sales stores

Estates - appraisals & sales

Eyeglasses, contacts (donate to)
 Eye Bank
 Funeral homes
 Lions Club
 Ophthalmologists
 Optometrists
 Prevent Blindness Association

Games, puzzles, toys (donate to)
 nursing homes
 day care centers
 adult day care centers
 nursery schools
 church schools

Hearing aids (donate to)
 Hear Now
  9745 E. Hampden Ave.
  Suite 300
  Denver, CO 80231-4923
  (303) 695-7797
  1-800-648-HEAR
  (303) 695-4860 TTY
 March of Dimes

If you have special items that you think someone would like, let your fingers do the walking in the phone book or online and find someone who can use the treasures you have. One woman had embroidered pillow tops with German phrases and figures. They weren't things that would have worked well at a sale, so she donated them to the local chapter of the German American Club. They were used there for a raffle.

Jewelry buyers

Letters, documents, photos—old (donate)
    colleges
    historical societies
    museums
    universities

Medical supplies/equipment (donate)
    American Cancer Society
    American Diabetes Association
    American Heart Association
    American Lung Association
    American Red Cross
    Homeless centers
    Hospice
    Local medical society
    Local hospital
    Related associations

Miscellaneous clothes/household belongings (donate)
    American Council for Blind
    American Veterans
    Disabled American Veterans (DAV)
    Goodwill
    Salvation Army
    Volunteers of America

Pet supplies (dog houses, crates, leashes, bowls, toys, old blankets/towels, etc.)
    (donate to Humane Society or other animal care/rescue organization)

Records, tapes, & cd's

Vintage clothing (sell/donate)
    consignment shops
    drama programs in schools/community

Wigs, hair pieces (donate to)
    American Cancer Society
    Hospice
    Leukemia and Lymphoma Society
    Local hospital

Purses and hats

These are very personal items. You might have a purse for every outfit/pair of shoes. Men might have hats/caps for every occasion. It is hard to part with even one. But you might have to because of space requirements. Go through and eliminate the ones that need repair (broken clasp, strap, spot on bill, too small, etc.). Next put in a stack the ones you use most often. Add the ones you can't live without. If you still have too many to take, repeat the process.

DEFINITIONS

With the development of more and more facilities for seniors to use when they downsize, the terms for identifying them have grown even more complex. It is important to look at the questions found earlier in this workbook to identify what you need/want. Some facilities offer a range of services so an individual can move in and be a fairly independent person but have the flexibility of moving to other areas of the same complex/campus as their needs change.

As you compare the various living arrangements, be sure to evaluate it as a long-term prospect. Look at the financing requirements. Some places require an admission fee when you move in. Is this a not-for-profit or for-profit organization, does it have financial stability, do you have to invest money, can you or your heirs get any refund? Can you get your deposit back if you change your mind? Once you move in, are you paying month-to-month or with a large or small by-in? Is there an 'estate' plan for lifetime care?

Is any of that amount refundable if you decide to leave or need to move for medical or other reasons?

Is the facility locally owned and operated? Is there a religious affiliation? Who is/are the responsible parties? Are there similar facilities in other communities in case you would need to move to another area of the country?

If you are selling your home and buying another, be sure to talk to your accountant/tax preparer for the tax implications. The equity you have in your home, if invested wisely, might provide the income you need to make a move.

....

Adult Day Care
Place for seniors to go during the day so they may either continue to stay in their own homes at night or with family members who work during the day. Meals, activities, and supervision are provided.

Apartment
Rental property, generally paid for in monthly installments; can have all or some of utilities provided; does not offer meals or other personal services.

Assisted Living
Apartment style living (mostly independent) with needed services provided such as meals, personal help, medications, housekeeping, etc.

Condominium
Individual owns living unit with monthly maintenance fee to cover outside/common area maintenance. Property outside living unit is jointly owned by all condo owners in complex.

Group Home
Place where seniors live with common areas (kitchen, living room, etc.) and with separate bedrooms; sharing household tasks and expenses.

House
Individual owns building and property. Responsible for all maintenance and utilities.

Memory Unit
Place for people with dementia or Alzheimer's disease, with staff trained and facilities designed to deal with special needs. Secure areas provided.

Nursing Home
Place for individuals who can no longer provide basic care for themselves. For those who need greater support for mobility, meals, medications, therapy and daily living tasks (physical and mental). Can be post-operative, rehabilitative or long-term. Recreation and crafts generally provided.

Patio Home/ Villa/ Garden Home
Generally one-floor plan with minimal yard and outside maintenance; individually owned. In some cases on the property of a 'retirement' community, but can be free-standing with no meals, cleaning, or other services provided.

Retirement Community/ Seniors' Residence
Building and/or complex where seniors reside in individual units (apartments or separate dwellings). Various arrangements are available for providing one or more meals, transportation, security, housekeeping, social activities and other amenities. Each facility has its own requirements for purchasing, renting or partial purchase (equity return).

Retirement Housing/ Community
Individual units that can be purchased like condos but built with seniors in mind. Age requirements for moving in; some services provided but generally no meals, medical, housekeeping, transportation, or activities provided.

Seniors' Residence
Units that are geared for seniors providing one or more meals, related services (housekeeping, security, etc.) and activities.

WHAT TO LOOK FOR?

When you visit a facility where you are considering moving, use this checklist to help you remember what to ask, what you found out and how to compare more than one place.

	Choice A	Choice B	Choice C
Date			
Name			
Address			
City/zip			
Phone			
Contact			
Type:			
retirement community			
independent living			
assisted living			
nursing care			
Alzheimer's unit (secure)			
Ownership:			
local			
chain/national/regional			
Number of units			
Total number of residents			
Ratio of women to men			
Average age			
Waiting list (yes/no)			
How long?			
Entry/admission fee			
Type accommodation			
high-rise			
1–4 stories			
elevators			
free-standing units			
cluster units			

	Choice A	Choice B	Choice C
Appearance:			
one building			
campus style			
landscaping			
neighborhood			
inviting entrance			
nicely decorated			
uncluttered			
home-like feel			
commercial feel			
nice smell			
well maintained			
Transportation:			
provided for medical			
provided for personal			
flexible			
unavailable			
Personal car:			
lot			
reserved parking			
secure parking			
covered parking			
garage/carport			
Staff:			
pleasant attitude			
treated with respect			
Residents:			
pleasant			
appropriate dress			
Dining:			
dress code at dinner			
appealing dining room			
1 meal daily (costs)			
2 meals daily (costs)			
3 meals daily (costs)			

	Choice A	Choice B	Choice C
assigned seating			
served cafeteria style			
served restaurant style			
served buffet style			
tray service (if required)			
standing meal times			
sufficient quantity served			
appetizing			
tasty			
other food options			
guest meals			
walkers allowed			
wheelchairs allowed			
separate dining for:			
assisted living			
nursing center			
Activities:			
exercise class			
indoor swimming			
outdoor swimming			
outings			
crafts			
bridge			
cards/bingo/games			
shuffleboard			
pool table			
exercise room			
tennis			
putting green			
bicycling			
lectures			
music area			
library			
shop area			
computer room			

	Choice A	Choice B	Choice C
chapel			
big-screen TV (lounge)			
onsite banking			
onsite convenience store			
special events			
community events			
gardening			
special occasion functions			
Maintenance/repairs:			
provided			
extra charge			
decorating provided			
personal decorating allowed			
Arrangements (cost):			
own			
buy-in (no ownership)			
rent			
living quarters close to dining area			
studio			
studio with kitchen			
studio with sitting area			
room without kitchen			
1 bedroom with bath			
2 bedroom, 1 bath			
2 bedroom, 2 bath			
deposit required			
refundable			
adequate closets			
patio/deck/balcony			
storage area			
cable TV (basic)			
extra charge			
flat linens provided			
telephone			

	Choice A	Choice B	Choice C
personal laundry service			
washer/dryer in unit			
laundry room available			
housekeeping:			
weekly			
every-other week			
monthly			
bath tub only			
shower only			
bath/shower combo			
grab bars			
emergency call system			
smoke detector			
carbon monoxide detector			
sprinkler system			
security staff			
handicapped accessible			
window treatments provided			
Medical/health office			
Scheduled podiatrist visits			
Counseling services			
Staff trained in CPR and first aid			
Staff/management on site 24 hrs			
Physicians:			
on-call			
own required			
available daily			
weekly			
none			
Pets allowed			
Resident council			
Guest accommodations			
Apartment available for trial use			
Chaplain			
Religious services conducted			

	Choice A	Choice B	Choice C
Beauty/barber services			
Smoking permitted (in personal areas)			
Smoking prohibited (in common areas)			
Other			
Other			
Other			
Other			

Notes

EVALUATING EXPENSES

When visiting the various facilities you are considering, decide how much you can afford.

Look at the expenses you pay each month in each of these categories. Write down your monthly income. With many of the facilities providing meals, maintenance, cable TV, property taxes, housekeeping services, you may find the monthly expenditure to be less than you are currently paying. But be sure to put a pencil to it. You don't want to make a move only to find that after a few months/years it is more than you want or can afford to pay.

Monthly rent/mortgage/condo fee	
Utilities water	
gas/electric (heating/air conditioning)	
basic cable TV service	
telephone (include long distance costs)	
Routine cleaning service	
Lawn/yard maintenance/snow removal	
Special cleaning (window washing, deck, etc.)	
Home upkeep (roof, furnace, gutter cleaning, etc.) average monthly amount from last five years	
Food (50%–65% of your average grocery bill)	
Property taxes	
Security system	
Insurance (homeowners)	
Other	
Total monthly expenses:	

- If you have saved **old toothbrushes** for those odd cleaning tasks... how many do you have? You can get by on a maximum of four. Put one near each sink and pitch the rest. (This is assuming you will still be getting new toothbrushes and having a replacement every six months or so.)

- Do you have **video tapes of programs** you have taped to watch later? It *is later.* Start a campaign to view those tapes a few at a time. Use the time when you might be watching reruns or channel surfing. Reuse the tapes from programs you don't want to save and label the ones you want to keep. (If you really want to be organized, make a list of the programs you have saved so you can find them quickly when you want to watch.) There probably are some programs you can't remember why you taped or that aren't on the tape you thought they would be! Be selective. Feel free to share special tapes with friends. (Another good tip is to give friends books, tapes, other small items and ask them to bring them to you in your new home. That way, you won't have to move them!)

- **Clothes**. What season is it now? If you are like most people, you have a few outfits that are your favorites. You feel the most comfortable in them and wear them the most often. What about all those other things taking up space in your closet? How many can you get rid of? Do they need laundering? Mending? Wrong color? Out of style? **When in doubt, throw it out.** If you didn't wear it last season, chances are you won't wear it this year either. This applies not only to hanging things but to sweaters and other chest of drawer and shelf things. You can simplify your life a lot by getting rid of the "extras."

- Do you have an accumulation of **bud vases and flower containers**? Many churches and nursing homes can put them to good use. Get the ones you won't need (all but a couple for your use) and call around to see who might like to have your leftovers.

Try to handle an item ONE TIME. Decide what should be done with it— keep, family, sell, donate, throw away— and then mark it.

MORE TIPS

- Have you kept **toys and books for your visiting grandchildren**? Have they outgrown the items you have? Ask them or their parents if there are any specific items they want and donate the rest to a homeless shelter or other needy group.

- Have you saved **every canceled check you've ever written**? You don't need to take them to your new home. If it makes you feel better to save a year or two, do. But pitch the rest. Same goes with old utility bills and other receipts. If there is a warranty involved, then save it. But if you saved it just to know how much you paid for something, this would be a good time to toss.

- If you are **decorating less for holidays, it might be time to let those decorations go**. If you have lots that you don't use and only a few you do, this would be a good time to keep them moving. You might have decorations for Christmas, Halloween, Thanksgiving, Easter, Passover, 4th of July, and even regional events. If you aren't using them, let someone else enjoy them.

- Have you been through your **medicine cabinet** lately? This is a great place for things to accumulate. If you have expired prescription drugs, check with your pharmacy about how/where to properly dispose of them. Please don't flush or simply put them in the trash. Some communities offer periodic "drug toss" events to help people dispose of out-of-date medicines.

- Do you have enough **gift wrap** on hand to wrap gifts for the graduating class at the local high school? Have you saved enough bows to circle your county? Do you have boxes of all sizes in case you need them? And what about tissue paper? Do you have enough of that to stuff a dozen gift-bags and still have some left over? Time to start using it! Don't buy more or save what you receive. Are you giving checks to family members for gifts now and don't even wrap gifts? Think about it.

*A*fter reading *MOVING FOR SENIORS: A step-by-step workbook*, you and your family should be able to see how your downsizing can be accomplished. It won't be easy, but with the techniques described here, it can be done with the least number of hassles possible. The best thing to remember is to break your project down into small segments so you aren't overwhelmed by it all. Solicit help from friends and family. (It is generally easier for outsiders to part with items that need to be tossed than for those with a sentimental attachment to things.)

Contracting a Senior Move Manager might be the easiest way to make your move. (It is generally easier for outsiders to be more objective when sorting through a lifetime of accumulations.)

If you will set a goal of so many hours each week and then break that down, just an hour a day will make a difference and you will see huge progress. Some days you will be inclined to do more, others, your schedule will dictate less. But making a move is a lot like eating an elephant. You do it, one bite at a time.

Do a drawer, the shelf in one closet, a cabinet, a box of 'treasures', but stay at it. Even if your move isn't for several years, you will feel better by doing the process in smaller increments, rather than in a rush.

Try to handle each item as little as possible. Group like things together (video tapes, books, figurines, etc.,) to make the packing and listing of those things easier. This can also cut down on the number of steps you have to make from room to room and up and down stairs.

If you can establish a calendar for when you want to make your move, you can set goals for what you need to accomplish daily/weekly/monthly until the move date. The hard part is deciding to begin. Remember that old proverb about "a long journey begins with the first step." Make that step toward a new home with treasures from your present home. Keep telling yourself it can be done and that you are going to do what you can to make it possible.

If you find your moving project is a little overwhelming and you need professional advice/assistance, check the
Smooth Transitions® website:
www.movingforseniors.com or the
National Association of Senior Move Managers (NASMM), www.nasmm.com for the name and number of a member near you.

The National Association of Senior Move Managers (NASMM) is a not-for-profit, professional association of organizations dedicated to assisting older adults and families with the physical and emotional demands of downsizing, relocating, or modifying their homes. The senior move industry is relatively new, but the challenge of transitioning an older adult is not. As the

National Association of Senior Move Managers
(NASMM)
99 Park Ave., Suite 202,
Clarendon Hills, IL 60514
877.606.2766
www.NASMM.com

only professional association in the country devoted to helping the rapidly increasing 55+ population with middle and later life transition issues, NASMM members are committed to maximizing the dignity and autonomy of all older adults.

MOVING for SENIORS:
A step-by-step workbook

by Barbara H. Morris

This hands-on workbook has the answers you need in making a move. It features questionnaires, checklists, suggestions, useful tips and resources to make downsizing easier for both you and your adult children. The resource can help you decide if (or whether) it is time to move, how to find a place to best meet your needs and budget, and how to find new homes for your treasures. *Moving for Seniors* makes it easier.

Order a copy for friends, relatives, or send one to your parents or children. Each copy is $15 including postage, tax and handling.

clip and send form with your payment to:
SMOOTH TRANSITIONS®
601 Briar Hill Road, Louisville, KY 40206-3011
(502) 897-9332   info@movingforseniors.com

Please make check payable to
SMOOTH TRANSITIONS®
or order online at www.movingforseniors.com

MOVING for SENIORS: *A step-by-step workbook*

Name

Address

City	State	Zip

Phone ( ) area code	Quantity	Total $ enclosed

SMOOTH TRANSITIONS LLC

Household Downsizing & Estate Dispersal

(502) 897-9332

SMOOTH TRANSITIONS is designed to provide individuals and families the emotional and physical assistance needed in making a change in living arrangements.

- Providing services for those who are considering a move for personal, family or medical reasons.

- Establishing short and long-term goals for living arrangements.

- Assessing present residence as well as assistance in finding alternative living arrangements when making a life change.

- Evaluating what items to keep and how best to dispose of other treasures accumulated over a lifetime.

- Helping families sort and disperse personal belongings with care, efficiency and attention to detail.

For out-of-town family members, **SMOOTH TRANSITIONS** provides peace of mind that someone is coordinating your family member's affairs with the personal attention you would give.

For more information or to see if there is a **SMOOTH TRANSITIONS** in your community, please contact:

SMOOTH TRANSITIONS
601 Briar Hill Road
Louisville, KY 40206-3011
(502) 897-9332
info@movingforseniors.com
www.movingforseniors.com

Your new floor plan

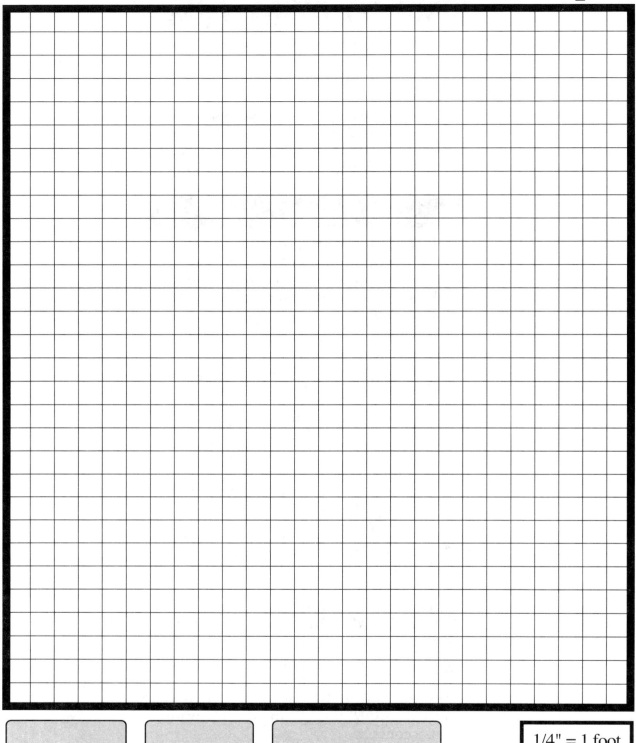

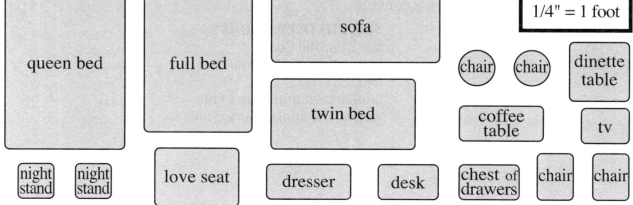

1/4" = 1 foot

BUSINESS START-UP

For those interested in starting a senior moving service, **Smooth Transitions**® offers two business models. One option is to become a **Licensee**. Cost is based on size of territory designated.

Licensee

This option includes:
- a protected territory
- business consulting
- rights to use the **Smooth Transitions**® name and logo
- rights to use artwork for brochure, business cards & stationery
- discounts on *Moving for Seniors* workbooks
- inclusion on *Moving for Seniors* website www.movingforseniors.com
- and more

Training Only

Those who would like to start a business but have a different business name they wish to use can purchase "Training Only". This includes:
- a *Smooth Transitions® Training & Operations manual*
- optional personal training
- discount on *Moving for Seniors* workbooks, phone consultation
- and more.

SMOOTH TRANSITIONS®LLC

For information on opportunities to start a *SMOOTH TRANSITIONS*® service in your community, please call.

SMOOTH TRANSITIONS®
601 Briar Hill Road
Louisville, KY 40206-3011
(502) 897-9332
info@movingforseniors.com
www.movingforseniors.com

Notes

> **Pare down tip!**
> Check below your sink, in your laundry area, pantry and other areas where you store cleaning items. You probably have your favorites plus an assortment of things you have tried but didn't like or don't use. Pass them along to someone who might want them or pitch. Pitch or pass <u>now</u>, not <u>later</u>. Do it now before the timer is running for that moving date.